Forever ON A SPANISH MOUNTAIN!

HOW 146 LIVES ENDED FOREVER ON A SPANISH MOUNTAIN IN TENERIFE

Vol I

STEPHEN BLOOM

Author's introduction

If you look up the accident that befell Dan Air flight 1008 on 25th April 1980 at Tenerife, you will find very little information. Not so other accidents involving aeroplanes. Look up the Mount Erabus accident in Antarctica, or the mid-air collision over Zagreb, or even the Staines air crash. You'll find some dedicated books, if you're interested like me. But others are strangely absent. Where is a proper dedicated book on the Tenerife collision of 1977, where 583 people died? Or the Basle air crash in 1973, where 108, mostly mothers with children, were killed?

Certainly I'll take up writing about those accidents next. But of Dan Air 1008 – very little information! This particular accident was blamed upon the flight crew by the Spanish investigating authorities – the *Comisión de Investigación de Accidentes e Incidentes de Aviación Civil,* or CIAIAC, who found four points of error apportioned to the British flight crew, and only one point of error apportioned to Spanish air traffic control. We will see later who was right when apportioning blame. Today we tend to find just causes, or corporate manslaughter.

Civilian aircraft accidents are usually always a case of blaming someone – nobody it seems wants to take responsibility for what happened. The Dutch, for example, tried their upmost to wriggle out of responsibility for the Tenerife ground collision in 1977, in which 583 lives were lost. Yet from the Spanish report, and air traffic tapes, it is clearly obvious that KLM Captain Jacob Louis Veldhuyzen van Zanten, the KLM chief flying instructor of all people, commenced his take off run in the belief that the Pan Am 747 had vacated the runway – and without takeoff clearance from air traffic control, despite the American crew warning air traffic that they were still taxying down the foggy runway.

The French, as another example and the operator of Basle airport back in 1973, tried in their report to blame the loss of 108 lives entirely upon the British flight crew – despite the air traffic controller, during a snow storm, not bothering to check the radar scope for the true location of Invicta 435, which had been driven off course by illegal radio transmissions that affected their navigational instruments *(see Vol II this series)*.

Believe me, I'm no expert in the field: no accident investigator nor pilot – in fact, I have just a passing interest in all things flying and flight simulation of the PC type – plus, I used to work in air traffic control during my days in the RAF at the London air traffic control centre (LATCC MIL) West Drayton in the early 1980's. But I feel that a fresh mind, looking over what evidence there is still available, can sometimes turn up new clues as to what happened.

Dan Air flight 1008 will be my first effort; perhaps the Tenerife ground collision and the Basle air crash with a Swiss mountain might follow in my portfolio. I hope things may be clearer, by the end of this book, as to what happened, why it happened, and not be just another blame game between Britain and Spain. *This book is dedicated to those killed and their relatives.*

- Stephen Bloom 2017 -

1

Oh this year I'm off to sunny Spain!

These are words to a well-known 1974 UK song sung by Sylvia Vrethammar – perhaps echoed by families and friends queuing at check-in at Manchester airport on the 25th April 1980. Flight 1008 was a charter from the chilly spring weather of the UK to the consistently warm climes of the Spanish Canary Isle of Tenerife. As the crow flies, it's just over 1600 nautical miles and about 4 hours' flight time.

As the passengers queued for boarding, five cabin staff must have been busy preparing for the arrival of their happy holiday makers. After a year of toil for most, a welcome spring break to an island where the average daily temperature rarely dropped below 70°C was but a short haul away. The Easter bank holiday in 1980 was Monday 7th April, therefore the children were still at school and most of those boarding G-BDAN, a Boeing 727 built in 1966, were most certainly on the whole adults.

Why mention this? Well, flight 1008 was so poorly documented that I could not even find the names of the five cabin crew on board, let alone 138 fare paying passengers! I examined pictures of the South Cemetery memorial to the 146 victims in Manchester, and the slates used are faded and almost unreadable. The only names I can give, excepting the flight crew of course, are as follows: Joan and Harry Game (sic), Brian and Sheila Francis, Deborah (sic) Bates aged 22, and Kim, Joyce, Nicola Valentine (and one other name obscured by grass growth).

Eight passengers or cabin staff! If anyone reading this knows of any of the other 130 passengers, or the five cabin crew, please contact me so that I can add them to an obituary. Meanwhile, in the cockpit of the Boeing 727 sat the three flight crew, going through their pre-flight checks. They supervised the loading of 49,800 lbs. (22604 kg) of jet fuel; thus the take-off weight of their aircraft was 167892 lbs. (76154 kg). All the figures were checked and double checked, before being signed off by the crew.

The captain for this flight is Arthur John Whelan (51), known as 'Red' to his colleagues due to his auburn coloured hair. Red had over 15,299 hours' total flight experience, of which 1912 hours' were on the Boeing 727. He also had undergone 58 previous flights into Tenerife's Los Rodeos* airport, the last time being just three months earlier in January 1980. In the previous 24 hours' he had rested. He hailed from Birmingham, and his distinct Brummy accent can be clearly heard on the cockpit voice recorder prior to the accident. There was a photo of Red in one of the newspapers at the time reporting the tragedy – I have sadly been unable to locate it anywhere.

* A new airport had opened in 1978 on south Tenerife, following the 1977 runway collision disaster at Los Rodeos – Reina Sofia airport (Queen Sofia Airport).

Assisting the captain on the flight deck is first officer (F/O) Michael John Firth (34). He hailed from Somerset and held a valid commercial pilot's license* with 3492 hours' total flight experience and 618 hours' on type; he had flown into Tenerife nine times previously and had rested the day before the accident.

* The co-pilot held a commercial pilot's license (CPL) whereas the captain held an air transport pilot's license (ATPL) – differences are very subtle but generally to get an ATPL requires on average 1500 hours' flight time.

The flight engineer (FE) on Dan Air 1008 was 34-year-old Raymond John Carey, hailing from Dartford. He held a valid flight engineers license. He had 3340 hours' total flight experience. I cannot determine how much time was spent on just the Boeing 727; his previous aircraft was the Comet 4. On the day before the accident he had worked five hours as standby flight engineer.

This is the experienced flight crew for Dan Air flight 1008. As for the aircraft itself, it was a Boeing 727 – 100/46 constructed in June 1966. The certificate of airworthiness was renewed in February 1980. Since construction, the aircraft had flown 30622 hours; the three engines since last overhaul had flown 9064 hours (1 engine), 11606 (2 engine) and 3750 (3 engine). There was nothing irregular in their operation or maintenance.

The aircraft was also fitted with various navigation aids, predominantly supplied by Collins; this included HF/VHF communications (radios), ADF (automatic direction finder), ILS / VOR (instrument landing system / VHF Omni-Range), DME (distance measuring equipment) and an ATC transponder. Also on board was a Bendix supplied Marker Beacon alerting system, an airborne search radar (weather radar) and a radio altimeter. Gables supplied the on board communications (pilot to pilot, cabin crew, etc). A Cracor supplied VLF Omega 7800 navigation system was also installed but not fully operational until it had been incorporated in the aircraft's radio certificate.

So now we are ready to taxy and take off from Manchester airport. Seatbelts fastened, seats in the upright position – there were no mobile phones of the type available today to switch off. Take off was from one of four runways: 05L/R (north-eastwards) or 23L/R (south-westwards). Since the flight was wholly routine until descent to Los Rodeos, nothing of the aircrafts departure or route was documented.

At 09:22 in the morning of Friday 25th April 1980 the Boeing 727 lifted off the runway at Manchester airport and took up a heading for the Spanish Canary Isles. The 138 fare paying passengers must have been beaming with the joyful thought of a few weeks in the sun, commencing in just a few hours' time. The cabin crew at some stage prepared a meal for their charges – probably a late breakfast, but possibly lunch too. The drinks trolley would have been busy satisfying the holidaymakers thirst. But for all those inside that pressurized tin can, they were never to enjoy sunshine again.

2

Arrival in the Tenerife area

As you relax in your cramped passenger seat, you probably wait with anticipation for that illusive drinks trolley to reach you. As usual, there are two trolleys pushed by stewardesses, both starting service at the opposite ends of the passenger cabin – your seat, of course, is right in the middle! Thirst quenching will have to wait a little longer, despite the dry recirculated air of the cabin. Outside the window, blue sky and sunshine greet you, with deep blue seas passing beneath. Close your eyes and relax; the stewardesses will be a while yet. Oh, and don't worry, I won't let you be on board at the end of this tragic flight.

Up front, your flight crew probably feel a little tired themselves. With modern mechanization and computers, flying a plane can be fairly simple and automated – just like driving a car, but with a vertical element. Your pilot comes into his own, and earns his pay, when things break down or go wrong. So, after the aircraft climbs to cruising level, the pilot is more or less monitoring things and recalculating fuel consumption until it is time to descend. Dan Air 1008 probably flew across Wales and Bristol, before crossing the channel and flying along the west side of France into Biscay.

Next it crossed Spain, and remained under Spanish control until handing over to Morocco air traffic. Finally, the aircraft would have been handed over to the Las Palmas control centre on the island of Grand Canary. Descent began under the auspices of Las Palmas. The vital time fast approaches now, for at 12:45 Las Palmas hands over Dan Air 1008 to Tenerife North Approach (called APP from now on). The aircrew finally call Tenerife APP at about 13:14, nearly seven minutes before the accident; there is no area radar at Tenerife north APP, so the aircraft comes under 'procedural control.'

There are a number of 'waypoints' along 'air corridors' approaching the island, and the pilots report by radio their location with regard to these waypoints. Over land, there are radio beacons of varying types that pilots use to fix their position. Dan Air is heading towards the VOR (VHF Omni-Range) type beacon called TFN, which is sited about 5.4 NMs (nautical miles) north-east of the airport. This marks the spot where the crew have to manoeuvre, ready for landing – in this case, on runway 12 (west to east approach).

The final six minutes of the flight were covered in the official accident report (HMSO 8/81). It would be better if I include the air traffic communication with the cockpit crew conversations, along with any pertinent information or comment by me (*in brackets/italics*). This chapter also includes some pictures of approach plates, the plot of the aircraft as deduced by Spanish investigators, and the accident scene.

So, the aircraft is now five minutes to impact and Las Palmas control have just handed Dan Air 1008 to Tenerife north approach control (APP). The time is 13:16. APP asks 1008 to descend and maintain flight level six-zero (6000 feet). The 727 was cruising at 10,000 feet until this moment. The crew acknowledge the order and commence their descent.

'Coming off with the power then,' said FE Raymond Carey to the crew.

APP – 'Report your DME reading please.' (*This is Distance Measuring Equipment – in conjunction with most VOR beacons, a reading to or from the beacon can be read in the cockpit by the crew*)

1008 – 'Er, we're reading seven DME Tango Fox November (TFN) and requesting the QFE please.' (*There are a number of barometric settings used on aircraft altimeters – the two main two are QNH (pressure at sea level) and QFE (pressure at a particular datum, in this case, the airfield). QNH is set when aircraft fly by 'flight levels,' and QFE is set when making an approach and gives height above the ground. 1008 was now seven miles from VOR TFN)*

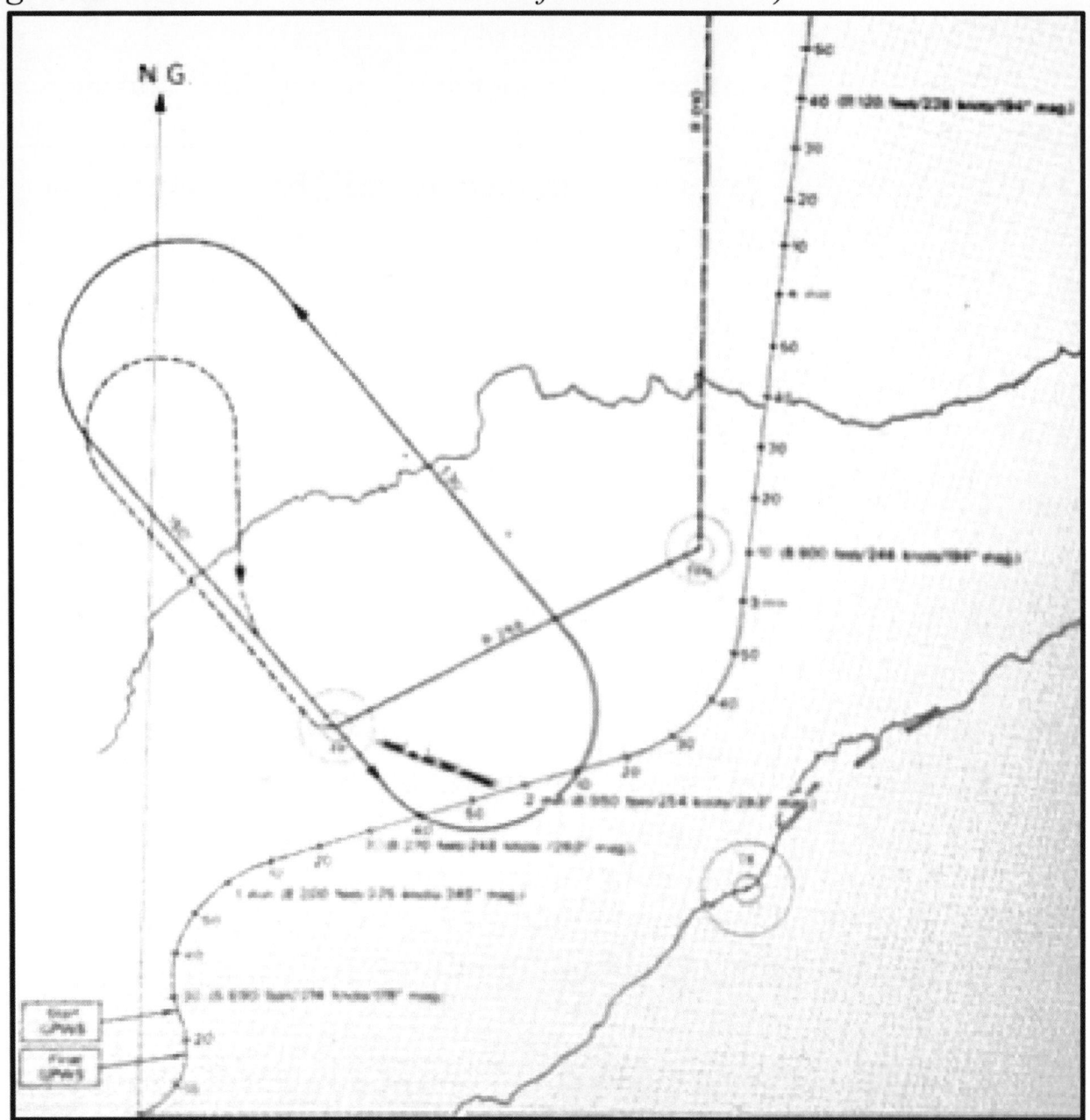

What happened? According to the official accident report, flight 1008 approached TFN too far east, continued south before making a tentative right turn towards FP, missed that locator entirely and continued west before starting an S shaped turn ending in disaster (courtesy HMSO accident report)

Los Rodeos airport – runway 12. FB is the marker beacon Dan Air 1008 never reached (courtesy Google Earth)

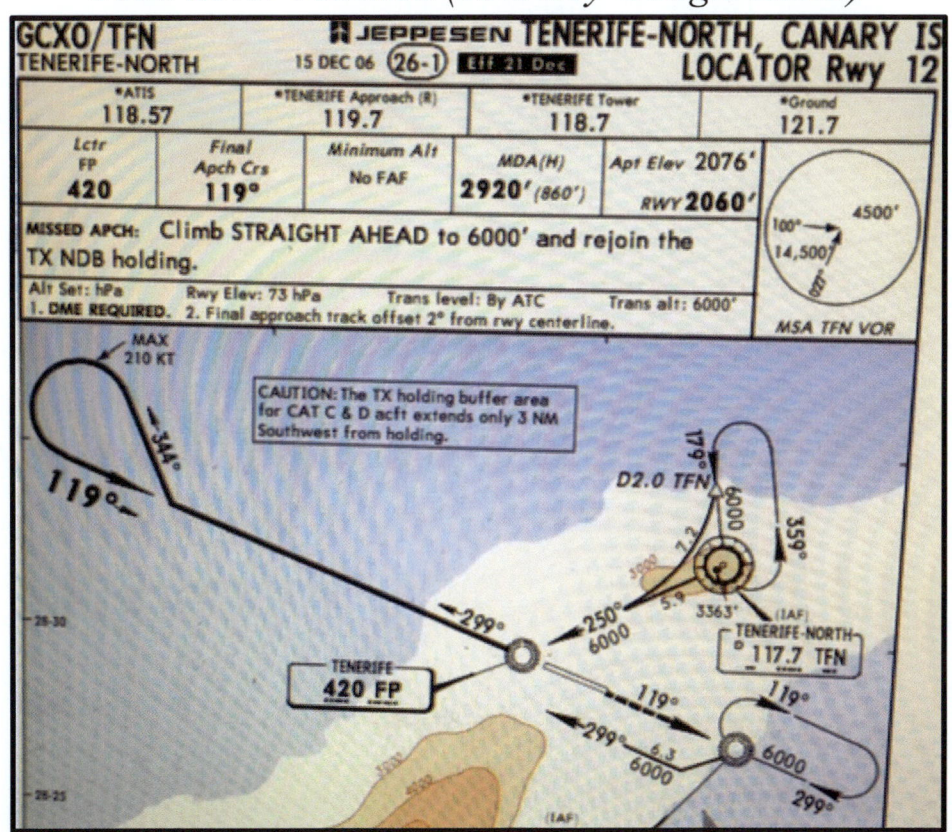

Locator approach plate – Dan Air 1008 was to approach from the north, pass over VOR TFN and then cross FP locator beacon, before heading out to sea and completing a tear drop turn before landing on runway 12 (courtesy Jeppesen).

APP – 'Nine four three.'

1008 – 'Nine four three, many thanks.' (*It is compulsory for aircrew to read back certain things to controllers, and this includes QFE. The pilots dial 943 millibars into their altimeters*)

P2 (Co-Pilot Michael Firth) 'Seventy millibars. You happy with that?'

P1 (Captain Red Whelan) 'Yeh. It's about right on this one. Ten for six then.'

P2 – 'Ten for six.' (*I'm not certain what the seventy millibars business was about – perhaps the differences between pressures – the ten for six means descending from 10000' for 6000'*)

P1 – 'You can put the ILS on your side. Might get it on a back beam for a lead in.'

P2 – 'And it's three oh two isn't it?'

P1 – 'Yeh.' (*This conversation refers to P2 dialling up the ILS (instrument landing system) on his side, and for runway 12 the frequency on his Nav 1 radio would be set to 108.7 MHz and a heading of 117° Magnetic. The heading of the ILS must be dialled in accurately, too. However, most ILS generally produce a 'back beam' – a reciprocal heading (often this is suppressed), and it was probably that referred to for a 'lead in'. The magnetic heading might be 297° but magnetic variation must also be taken into account, too, and would be added or subtracted.*

An instrument landing system (ILS) consists of several components: a localizer beam LOC (lateral movement to the runway centre line), a glide slope GS (usually a 3° approach angle to the touch down point) and position marker beacons (usually outer marker OM, middle marker MM and sometimes inner marker IM). The frequency dialled in is for the localizer and varies from location to location; the GS and marker beacons are 'matched' and don't need to be dialled in)

APP – 'One-zero-zero-eight, for your information (Quebec) Foxtrot Echo (QFE) on runway one-two is nine four one.'

1008 – 'Roger nine four one for one-two thanks.'

13:17.41 – FE – 'That's what I reckoned it should be by calculation.'

P1 – 'I won't go out the full procedure if you know because it takes you way out to sea on this.' (*The captain refers to an approach plate, like the Jeppesen plate above, where on a heading of 299° the aircraft goes well out to sea before commencing a tear drop turn back onto a heading for runway 12*)

APP – Iberia siete-uno-uno, notifique compleiando curva de procedimiento. (*Iberia seven-one-one, notify completing curve procedure – APP talking to aircraft Iberia 711. Communications should always be conducted in English, the international language of ATC*)

IB711 – Notificard, Iberia siete-uno-uno. (*Report, Iberia seven one-one – this likely refers to the tear drop procedure, prior to IB711 landing on runway 12*)

MORSE CODE IDENT – (*The ILS identifier 'ITF' sounds in the cockpit – the crew must identify the correct ILS before attempting an approach*)

P2 – 'ITF three-oh-five is in my box – three-oh-two, I'm sorry excuse me.'

13:18.15 – P1 – 'Just about to go overhead, going for.'

P2 – 'Two five out of here.' (*Here the co-pilot mentions that ITF (for the back beam 'lead in') on heading 302° is set his side; he corrects his initial error where he states 305°. The captain then remarks that they are just about to pass overhead VOR TFN. From the accident report, it is clear that they passed east of that beacon, and not overhead it, probably by one mile*)

13:18.41 – HP (another aircraft, Hapag-Lloyd 542) – 'Tenerife buenas tardes Hapag-Lloyd five four two.' (*Good afternoon*)

APP – 'Five four two good afternoon report ready.'

HP542 – 'Wilco.'

13:18.48 – 1008 – 'Dan Air one-zero-zero-eight has just passed the Tango Fox November (TFN) heading for the er Fox Papa.'

13:18.54 – APP – 'Roger the er standard holding overhead Foxtrot Papa is inbound heading one five zero turn to the left call you back shortly.' (*Here's a vital communication, like similar misunderstood instructions in 1977 at the same airport (resulting in two jumbo jets colliding on the runway and 583 deaths), that the experienced crew needed to understand. Note that a few 'er' symbols now creep into the conversation from both aircrew and air traffic controller*)

13:19.01 (error of time in the accident report) – 1008 – 'Roger Dan Air one-zero-zero-eight.' (*Here the Spanish and British investigators differed in opinions – an order to do something should have been read back by the crew to be sure there were no ambiguity or error – the flight crew did not read back, and air traffic control did not query why*)

3

Pull up! Pull up!

On board Dan Air 1008, the flight crew had just passed east of VOR TFN and were supposed to turn right towards the FB locator beacon situated 0.6 NMs from the touch down point of runway 12.

13:19.03 – P1 – 'Inbound one five zero to your left.'

    P2 – 'One five zero left yeah.'

    P1 – 'That's an odd sort of one the runway….'

13:19.10 – P1 – 'One to go.'

    P2 – 'One to go.'

    FE – 'One to go.' (*At this moment, 1008 had turned onto a southwest heading and was nearly at 6000 feet, but travelling at 254 kts. It is normal procedure throughout the world to fly below 250 kts when under 10,000 feet. Here the aircraft is about 2.5 NMs from FB, which was on its right, and travelling above permitted speed – way too fast for tight manoeuvres*)

13:19.17.5 – P2 – 'No I'm not er suppose it's alright.'

13:19.27 – P1 – 'I'll just turn straight round left onto one five zero when I go overhead then.' (*There is a ten second delay here before P1 spoke this to P2 – the captain is clearly confused by the controller's 'the standard holding overhead Foxtrot Papa' instruction*)

    P2 – 'Yes.' (*Reading this communication with air traffic control, the controller (Justo Camin Yanes, 34) had spoken the words 'Roger the er standard holding overhead Foxtrot Papa is inbound heading one five zero turn to the left call you back shortly.' At no time does he actually instruct 1008 to take up the hold; it only advises where the hold is situated if required. It might also explain why the crew did not read back the instruction and why Justo Yanes did not ask if they understood what he was saying. The crew should have continued with their approach at 6000 feet – heading to FP, then outbound on a heading of 299° at a maximum speed of about 210 kts, until commencing the tear drop turn*)

13:19.33 – P1 – 'The only thing is we're hmmm we're just about to miss it ha-ha it's too close.' (*The captain refers to missing the FP locator beacon*)

13:19.37.5 – P2 – 'Would you like the other one on the Fox Papa as well as for this?'

P1 – 'If you put them both on as we're going to hold yeh.' (*At this critical time P2 asks if the captain would like the FP information showing on his instruments too, and the captain says yes. Their conversation shows that the crew now believe they have been instructed to take up a hold at FP (despite such a hold being un-published on any chart). They had already missed the FP locator beacon too. Under such conditions the crew should have broken off the approach and gone around again for another attempt*)

13:19.40 – P1 – 'That's er that's the foxtrot papa now.'

P2 – 'Yep.'

13:19.51 – 1008 – 'Dan Air one-zero-zero-eight is foxtrot papa level at six zero (*6000 feet*) taking up the hold.'

13:19.57.5 – APP – 'Roger.' (*The crew now confirm they are going to take up the hold, but the controller simply replies 'roger.' Since he had no radar, he did not know where the aircraft was. In fact, they were directly south of FP at this time, at a very fast 248 kts and heading 263°, not turning north towards FP*)

<u>1 minute 20.5 seconds to disaster.</u>

13:20.02 – FE – 'That's the fuel.'

13:20.12 – P2 – 'Bloody strange hold isn't it?'

P1 – 'Yes doesn't isn't parallel with the runway or anything.'

13:20.17.5 – APP – 'Iberia siete-uno-uno notifique abandonando cinco mil.' (*Iberia 711 notify leaving five thousand*)

    P2 – 'It's that way isn't it?'

    FE – 'That is a three isn't it?'

13:20.21 – Iberia 711 – 'Libre cinco mil, ahora, estamos en curva de procedimiento.' (*Leaving five thousand now, we are in curve process – in other words, commencing their approach after the tear drop procedure*)

    P2 (to FE) – 'Hmm.' (*Just what the crew refer to was never fully established. Most likely something on an approach plate. At no time did the captain brief the crew on the approach procedure for Los Rodeos, which was a serious omission*)

    FE (to P2) – 'That is a three isn't it?' (*Repeats question*)

    P2 – 'Yes well the hold's going to be here isn't it?' (*Both junior officers appear confused now by the number three on a plate, and the location of the unpublished hold – to such an extent, in my opinion, to have become seriously distracted as to the aircraft's current location. They were likely in thick cloud by this time, too. They were, in fact, just 52 seconds from disaster and flying at 6200 feet, heading 245° and slowing to 225 kts.*

The pilot flying (probably the captain) had started to turn left, instead of right to FP. It can only be that the controller's words 'roger the er standard holding overhead Foxtrot Papa is inbound heading one five zero turn to the left' gave the impression to the captain that he must turn left onto a heading of 150° - which might be correct if they were actually over or north of FP. The accident report indicates at this time they had missed FP by at least 2000m and had entered a gentle left hand turn, away from FP locator, whilst the aircraft slowed)

13:20.25.5 – APP – 'Recibido. Break.' (*Transmission received (from Iberia 711). Break means the controller has finished with that aircraft and will talk to another. All this conversation and radio transmissions happened rapidly*)

13:20.26 – APP – 'Dan Air one-zero-zero-eight recleared to five thousand on the Quebec Foxtrot Echo (QFE) and Quebec November Hotel (QNH).'

13:20.33 – 1008 – 'Roger, cleared down to five thousand feet on the one zero one three (QNH of 1013 millibars), Dan Air one-zero-zero-eight.' (*Because Iberia 711 had just vacated 5000 feet, the controller cleared Dan Air down to that level. Neither crew nor controller knew where the aircraft was. The controller probably believed that 1008 was taking up or already in his unpublished hold, whereas the pilots did not know where they were so turned left towards heading 150°, as the controller said. This was a fatal mistake, for several reasons that will follow shortly*)

13:20.39 – APP – 'Roger.'

13:20.41 – P1 – 'Hey…did he say it was one five zero inbound?'

13:20.46 – P2 – 'Inbound yeh.'

   P1 – 'That's….'

13:20.46.5 – APP – 'Hapag-Lloyd five four two are you ready?' (*To take off*)

13:20.48 – P1 – 'I don't like that.'

   P2 – 'They want us to keep going more round don't they?'

13:20.49.5 – 'Affirmative Hapag-Lloyd five four two is ready.'

13:20.50.6 – GPWS audio commences – Pull up! Pull up! (*Ground proximity warning system. The aircraft was now heading due south (178° Magnetic) at 5690 feet altitude and 214 kts when the GPWS alarm sounded*)

13:20.52 – APP – 'The wind is one three zero, zero five (130/05), cleared for take-off runway one two.' (*The controller has cleared Hapag-Lloyd for take-off. He's controlling three aircraft – 1008, 711 and 542*)

   P1 – 'Okay, overshoot.'

13:20.56 – P1 – 'He's taking us round to the high ground.'

13:20.57.5 – P2 – 'Yeh.'

13:21.00.5 – GPWS audio ceases.

13:21.01 – P1 – 'Watch my, er, eepers.' (*EPR Engine pressure ratios*)

13:21.03 – P2 – 'I suggest a heading of one-two-two actually and er take us through the overshoot ha.' (*Where P2 gets 122° from is not clear, but I hazard a guess that the ILS overshoot for runway 12 is 119° and by adding magnetic variation, suggests 122°. When the alarm ceased, the aircraft began a hard bank to the right, instead of continuing left onto the co-pilot's suggested heading*)

    FE – 'Let's get out of here.'

13:21.07 – P1 – 'He's taking us round to high ground.' (*Repeats*)

13:21.08 – P2 – 'Yeh.'

13:21.13.5 – 1008 – 'Er, Dan Air one-zero-zero-eight, we've had a ground proximity warning.'

13:21.16.5 – FE – 'Bank angle. Bank angle!'

13:21.18 – IMPACT (*At the moment before impact the aircraft had been level at about 5500 feet for ten seconds, then descended slightly to 5450 feet during the bank, with a recorded airspeed of 258 kts and a heading of 253°. There was no attempt to climb out, probably because the GPWS had stopped, indicating no high ground, but the right hand bank reached about 40°, hence the flight engineer calling out 'bank angle' as he was obliged to do should the bank exceed 30°. The pitch angle of the plane was reduced when the GPWS ceased*)

4

Death on a mountain

1008 – 'Er, Dan Air one-zero-zero-eight, we've had a ground proximity warning.'

APP – 'Station calling…'

APP – 'Iberia siete-uno-uno notifique establecido en final.' (*Iberia seven-one-one notify set on finals*)

IB711 – 'Iberia seven-one-one notify set on final.

APP – 'Iberia siete-uno-uno autorizado a aterrizar pista doce, viento uno tres cero cinco… autorizado a aterrizar Iberia siete-uno-uno.' (*The controller clears Iberia 711 to land on runway 12. Dan Air should be circling above it at 5000 feet*)

APP – 'Dan Air one-zero-zero-eight, your position in the holding?'

APP – 'Ah Dan Air one-zero-zero-eight, Tenerife, request your position in the holding?'

Blank silence on the airwaves. The weather at Los Rodeos at the time was quite fine; not so in a south-west direction from the airport, where there was a small layer of cloud of 2/8 at 1000m, a second layer of between 4/8 and 6/8 1500m – 2000m and with tops at 10,000m – in other words, thick cloud in the mountain region. 8/8 is full cloud cover. Perhaps amongst the strewn wreckage, investigators found the tattered remains of the approach plates used by the crew? Above is one typical chart for ILS runway 12 at Los Rodeo. In the top right corner is a circle with various degrees/numbers inside it.

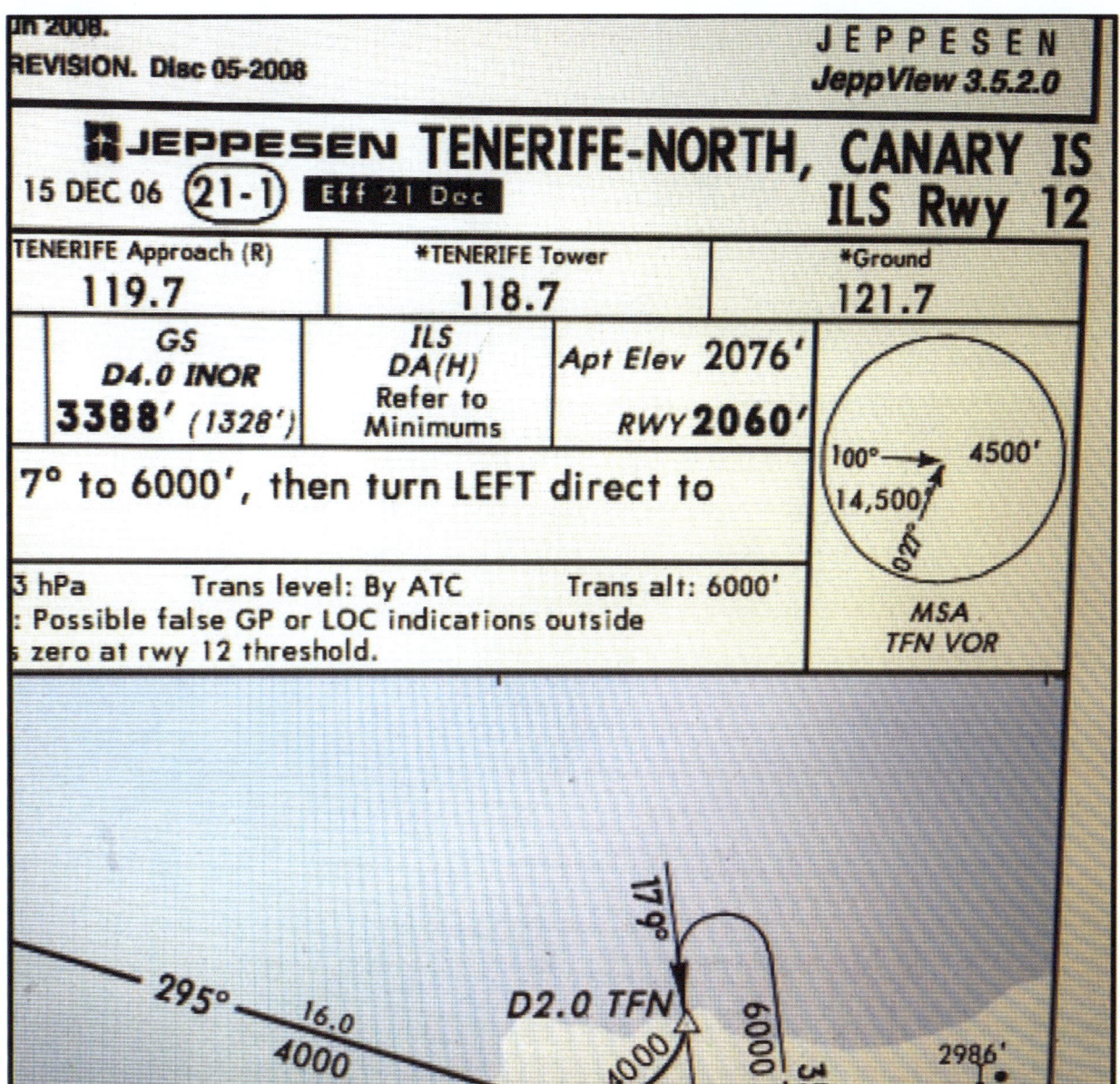

Chart showing Minimum Safe Altitudes (MSA) (courtesy Jeppesen)

You can see that between 027° and 100° (anti-clockwise) the minimum safe altitude (MSA) is 4500 feet. That is in the region of the airport. But between 100° (clockwise) and 027°, however, the MSA is 14500 feet. That is the region of the mountains on Tenerife. That is where Dan Air 1008 ended up.

The aircraft struck trees and rock at an altitude of 5450 feet above mean sea level (amsl) just 38m below the summit of this mountain, known locally as *Pico del Chiriguel*. The slope faced 33° towards the north-east. There is a valley between two peaks here, one peak being 4300 feet amsl, and another peak, the disaster peak, at 4800 feet – a valley between peaks explains how the GPWS activated as Dan Air crossed the first peak (4300 feet) but then deactivated as the aircraft crossed that valley. The steepness of the second peak, standing at angle of 30°, minus the angle of attack of the aircraft (about 10° nose up), gave a combined angle of 20°, which did not allow enough time for the GPWS to warn the crew a second time.

The aircraft broke up upon impact, as you would expect when such a heavy object slams into a mountain at 258 kts – that's 298 mph. Part of the cabin behind the wings, with the tail, continued some several hundred metres further on, before disintegrating and leaving a second trail of seats and their occupants – this was called scar two.

The main wreckage trail was measured as a long 350 metres in length, crossing the increasing slope obliquely to a height of about 60 metres from the initial impact point, and to a width of 200 metres. Much of this wreckage had rolled back down the slope again. This was called scar one.

It included much of the wings, the engines and left hand undercarriage – also the elevators, stabilizers and parts of the cockpit. Scar one continued with more cockpit parts, passenger baggage, nose landing gear, the wing centre section, further bits of the wings and stabilizer sections – the final parts consisted of fuselage mid and rear sections and electronics bay components.

Scar two extended for 250 metres, climbing 15 metres to the top of a ridge before descending 45 metres the other side and crossing a road track. A village on a bearing of 039° and 2 kms from the crash site reported burnt fragments and material blown over it from the accident. The actual site was heavily saturated with aviation fuel, and small fires had broken out in places.

Minute examination of the area by mostly Spanish investigators did uncover much evidence as to the state of the aircraft at impact. Most parts of all three engines were identified, and revealed that they were at high power at impact. The thrust reversers were found in the normal forward thrust positions. The control surfaces of the aircraft were mainly destroyed, although the tail jack assembly showed 5° nose up trim – quite to be expected.

It was not possible to determine fully whether the flaps/leading edges/kruger flaps on the wings were extended – all evidence pointed to them being retracted, as was to be expected. Parts of the cockpit instrumentation was also found. The Nav 2 box, for example, was set to 110.30 MHz, which is the ILS frequency for runway 30 at Los Rodeos – ITF. Nav 1 was set at 112.45 MHz, which I can't find – the nearest is 112.9 MHz at Las Palmas, Grand Canary. It's possible it moved during the crash. I would expect it to be set for the ILS for the runway – 108.7 MHz.

The altimeter was set at 1012.5 millibars (not 1013) and showed 5300 feet. Both the cockpit voice recorder (CVR) and the flight data recorder (FDR) were recovered intact and sent away for analysis. Half of the seat belts recovered were fastened, and most of the others had probably been opened by rescue personnel. Of 146 people on board, only 52 could be recovered intact and repatriated home. That's 35.6%, and sadly for the rest, they could not be identified and recovered, including the three flight crew members. There was nothing in their recent medical history, however, to suggest any of them were unfit for duty on the day of the crash.

Search and rescue was provided by the Spanish Rescue Aerial Service and the Gardia Civil (police); however, because the aircraft was not on the course expected by air traffic control and fog clung to the mountain region, it was not until 20:00 hours that the wreckage was found – that's more than six hours after Dan Air disappeared! The woody mountain slope was cordoned off and only a few bodies recovered before night fall. The following day, work began to recover all the bodies, and it took a further forty-eight hours before accident investigators could look over the site.

All airport radio aids were tested and found to be working satisfactorily; there was also no interference detected from amateur radio operators or overhead electrical cables. The aircraft's GPWS was examined closely by investigators and the manufacturer – this was a Litton design, built by Marconi Avionics and worked in conjunction with a Bendix radio altimeter. The system provides warnings to the crew in five modes under the following situations:

1 excessive rate of descent with respect to terrain – radio height above terrain versus barometric altitude sink rate
2 excessive closure rate to terrain – radio height versus closure rate
2a flaps not in landing configuration, landing gear up or down
2b landing configuration
3 altitude loss before acquiring 700 feet terrain clearance after take-off or a missed approach
4 flight into terrain with less than 500 feet terrain clearance not in landing configuration
5 excessive glide slope deviation

The GPWS on the aircraft operated only once; this lasted for 10 seconds, from 27 seconds to 17 seconds prior to impact, and occurred when the aircraft was 1500 feet above terrain (the first ridge peak) and for five seconds had a closure rate of 6000 feet per minute with that peak. The system deactivated after the first peak, due to the deep valley just beyond. As the aircraft crossed this valley, the second, fatal slope and ridge peak approached; the terrain closure rate started to increase but before the system could operate again, the aircraft slammed into the mountain.

5

So what went wrong?

Investigators quickly concluded that there was nothing wrong with the aircraft, and so attention tuned to the cockpit voice recorder, flight data recorder and air traffic control tapes. The Spanish air traffic controller, Justo Camin Yanes, first spoke to Dan Air at 13:14.33 after the aircraft called him from Las Palmas control. 1008 was at FL110 and just 14 NMs from TFN VOR beacon. The aircraft, in reality, was still descending to FL110 and 16 NMs from TFN at 280 kts (322 mph).

Yanes responded by clearing Dan Air from TFN to FP locator beacon at FL110, to expect runway 12, and most importantly, he added the words 'no delay.' The crew read back the instruction, leaving out the words 'no delay' and asked for the weather, which was passed. The airport was experiencing drizzle at the time. Was the controller busy at this time? No, for he had only one other aircraft ahead of Dan Air, IB711 which was a slower aircraft, and later HP542, which was ready to take off.

IB711 was now at 5000 feet, so the controller cleared 1008 down to 6000 feet. He also asked for the DME and Dan Air replied that they were 7 NMs from TFN. The FDR revealed the distance to be between 7.5 and 9 NMs from TFN. 1008 then passed the beacon but did not report it to ATC for a further 33 seconds. The CVR revealed no conversation in the cockpit to account for the late reporting of TFN; further, the aircraft speed continued to increase.

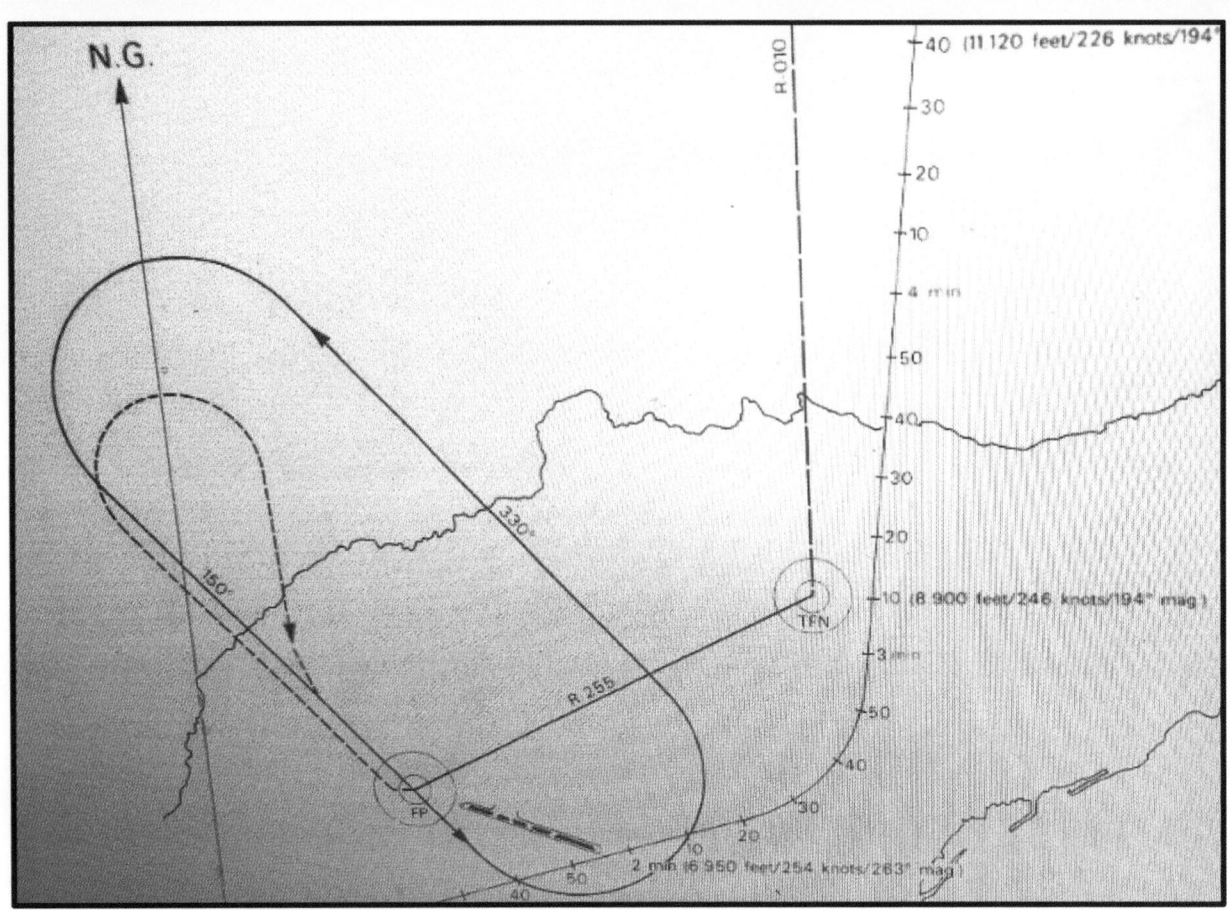

Approach: from TFN beacon, a right turn onto 255° to approach the FP locator beacon – Dan Air never completed this simple manoeuvre (courtesy the accident report)

ATC next issued information regarding the 'standard' holding over FP, which was inbound heading 150°, turn to the left. The crew acknowledged this but did not read back. Instead, they continued on a heading of 263° instead of 255° (for FP beacon), at 6200 feet (altitudes are acceptable to ± 300 feet) and exceeding the speed limit at 254 kts (should be slower than 250 kts at that height).

During a period now of 56 seconds, with no ATC transmissions, the crew discussed the standard holding over FP issued from the controller, during which their aircraft continued on its erroneous and dangerous course towards an area with an MSA of 14500 feet. They were certainly confused by several things: an unpublished holding procedure over FP that had no navigation chart; the earlier transmission

26

from ATC regarding there being 'no delay,' and the actual instruction from ATC of inbound 150°, turn to the left.

During the cockpit discussions, navigation of the aircraft was neglected. The sentence 'one to go' was said three times at this stage – I can only presume they meant one nautical mile to go to FP locator beacon. The aircraft was now at 6270 feet, at 248 kts (285 mph) and still heading 263°. However, using the investigation map of the plotted flight path, the aircraft was never closer than about 1.6 to 1.9 NMs from FP. This was never commented upon by Spanish investigators.

The next error by the crew followed immediately, with the captain saying 'I'll just turn straight round left onto one five zero when I go overhead then,' to which the co-pilot replied 'yes'. Neither man seems to have considered the consequences of doing what the captain said; neither did the F/O nor FE query the captain's suggestion or did the captain make it clear this was what they would do – only he says with some doubt and more like a suggestion, 'I'll just turn straight round left…then.' In attempting this left hand manoeuvre, more time was wasted debating whether it was the right thing to do whilst that MSA area of 14500 feet rapidly approached; surely a quick radio call to ATC would have cleared things up?

The crew next confirmed to each other that they had missed the FP locator marker. The aircraft was travelling way too fast to perform any significant manoeuvre other than a gradual left or right hand turn. The co-pilot appeared to sound a little anxious when they missed FP, and probably tried to bring it to the captain's attention by selecting FP on the captain's ADF set (Automatic Direction Finder – works in conjunction with NDBs, or Non-Directional Beacons). Dan Air was now flying blind, in cloud, and heading further away from FP and the airfield.

The F/O next reported the aircraft taking up the hold; ATC simply replied 'roger' and did not query why they were doing so, since he had not instructed them to do it, only advised them of it. It was a further 20 seconds or 2 NMs after reporting taking up the hold before the aircraft began to deviate further to the left. Further doubts from the F/O now followed when he said 'bloody strange hold isn't it?' The captain confirmed that it was so, since it wasn't parallel with the runway (117° for an ILS approach to runway 12 – the hold was supposedly 150°, a difference of 33°).

For a few moments the F/O and the FE discussed between them this hold, which was interrupted by ATC clearing 1008 from 6000 to 5000 feet 'on the Quebec Foxtrot Echo (QFE) and the Quebec November Hotel (QNH).' This was an error on behalf of ATC, since it should never have been given in this form (both QFE and QNH together) in case the aircrew selected the wrong datum. As it was, they selected the correct datum (QNH) and would have only used QFE once established on final approach.

Unless over the sea, or within the 27° - 100° MSA circle (4500 feet), then the crew should have warned ATC that they were entering a MSA of 14500 feet, and that such a descent was dangerous. The penny now dropped for the captain when he said suddenly 'hey, did he say it was one five zero inbound?' The F/O replied 'inbound, yeh.' The captain exclaimed that he didn't like that. He never said why, and the F/O said 'they want us to keep going more round, don't they?'

150° inbound. You fly the aircraft on a heading of 150° until reaching FP, where you turn to the left. Until that moment, the aircraft was manoeuvring too fast and in cloud to the left, in a vain attempt to fly a heading of 150° *away* from the FP locator! The conversation broke off when the GPWS sounded for the next 10 seconds, warning the crew to pull up. The captain stopped his left hand turn and ordered an overshoot, telling his colleagues that ATC was taking them around to high ground.

The aircraft started a turn to the right; in doing so it crossed a valley and the GPWS ceased warning. The co-pilot next suggested a heading of 122°, and how he came to that figure I cannot say, since it required a continuous left hand turn whereas the captain had just initiated a new right hand turn. The captain chose to continue his right hand turn, however, obviously convinced that the previous left hand turn was leading them into a mountainous region.

How the hold should have been done – from TFN heading 255° then at FP turn right and commence circling with left hand turns at FP (white lines). How it went (red lines). (courtesy Google Earth)

There were just a few seconds left for the captain to radio ATC and inform the controller that they had received a GPWS warning. As he was finishing his sentence, the FE called out 'bank angle – bank angle.' The aircraft then ploughed into the mountain side, in fog, and disintegrated, killing all on board. It was Dan Air company procedure, as mentioned earlier, for the FE to call out 'bank angle' should the angle for any reason exceed 30°. Even so, it still took 15 seconds for the FE to warn the captain when the bank started to exceed 30°.

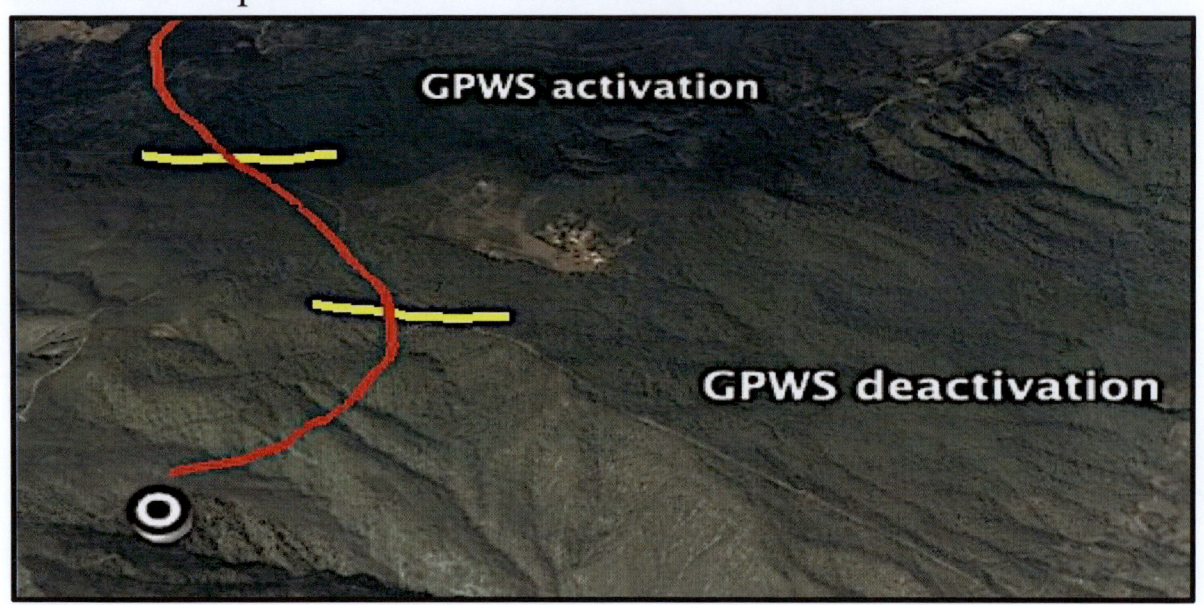

What happened – 1008 passed TFN to the east, rather than overhead, then crossed runway 30 threshold at 6000' heading 263°; missed FP by about 1.5 NMs, then began a left turn into a mountainous region with a MSA of 14500' – the GPWS activated for 10 seconds then deactivated just before collision (courtesy Google Earth)

6

Blame game

Many of the reasons for this appalling accident, as is usually the case, come down to a number of factors, and not just one thing. IB711, a slow moving propeller driven Fokker F27, was just descending from 6000 feet to 5000 feet ahead of Dan Air 1008. When 1008 reported TFN earlier than expected, probably due to its continuous high speed, the controller realized that the B-727 would quickly catch up with the F27, so he immediately thought of holding back 1008 until sufficient distance was maintained.

The proper procedure would be to hold 1008 at the VOR TFN, which was a very accurate type of navigation aid compared to the FP locator. This the controller did not do. He could not maintain lateral separation between the B-727 and the F27 because the Fokker was too slow. The only course of action was vertical separation, in this case 1000 feet between aircraft. 1008 had to go somewhere and had already passed TFN, so the only alternative, short of sending it back to Las Palmas control, was the unpublished hold above FP.

But because of its high speed, it took only 63 seconds for 1008 to pass TFN and report taking up the hold at FP. Why did the controller instruct 1008 to descend further to 5000 feet, when in fact it was in an area with a MSA of 14500 feet? Having no radar, he could not see where 1008 actually was, and he had only the procedural reports of the pilots to help him. He was expecting, if the hold was being taken up, for 1008 to reach FP on a heading of 255° from the east, and then take up a standard entry segment by heading 330° before turning left onto

150° back towards FP; thereafter, turn to the left and head out to sea again on the reciprocal heading (for 150° inbound) of 330°.

The controller had no reason to believe that 1008 was anywhere other than at FP heading out to sea; thus he cleared the aircraft down to 5000 feet when IB711 started its approach by leaving that level. A standard holding pattern, according to international air law (promulgated by ICAO) is always 'turns to the right, unless specified otherwise.' In this instance, the controller specified the direction of turn but made a grievous error by saying 'turn to the left' instead of 'turns to the left.' This one letter difference confused the crew of 1008, and yet they never challenged the instruction.

The investigators commented also on the speed of the aircraft after it passed TFN, which was close to 250 kts (287 mph), the imprecise navigation of not flying overhead TFN but to the east of it by about .79 NMs, and missing completely FP by about 1.59 NMs then not taking up the 255° radial. It seems to me that the crew had not briefed nor prepared in advance for the approach, which really should have been complete before descent begins. When passing east of TFN, the crew waited, inexplicably, for a further 33 seconds before reporting it to ATC.

According to investigators and the FDR, the procedure for an avoidance action in the circumstances of a GPWS activation was to achieve a best rate of climb – but this never happened, principally because the captain continued his turn to the right, heavily banked, rather than level the wings, with the result that 1008's altitude continued to descend slightly rather than climb away. As a result, the investigators had nine major findings, five major causes, and made three recommendations regarding the accident. The British investigation team then added an addendum to the Spanish report. Below is an abbreviated version.

<u>Findings of the Spanish investigating team</u>
1 The crew were properly qualified, experienced and medically fit.

2 The ATC controller was properly qualified, experienced and medically fit.

3 The aircraft had a valid certificate for airworthiness, registration and maintenance. It had been maintained in accordance with the approved maintenance schedule.

4 The captain did not follow the correct flight path after passing TFN and did not know his exact position, particularly after he reported passing FP.

5 ATC should have instructed the aircraft to hold at TFN.

6 Since the hold at FP was unpublished, the information furnished by ATC was incomplete.

7 The crew had little time to assimilate the information on the hold at FP and although they did not understand it, they did not ask for clarification.

8 The captain should have paid more attention to his navigation, in order to maintain a proper safe altitude in relation to the terrain, particularly as he was not being monitored by radar.

9 The co-pilot did not check or query the operations being carried out by the captain, as required by the company operations manual, with the result that the required co-operation between the crew did not occur.

Causes

The cause of the accident was that the captain, without taking account of the altitude at which he was flying, took the aircraft into an area of high terrain, and thereby failed to maintain a safe height above the terrain as he was required to do. The following were contributory factors:

1 Carrying out a manoeuvre without having it clearly defined.

2 Imprecise navigation by the captain which reveals that he was disorientated.

3 Lack of teamwork between captain and co-pilot.

4 The short time between the information on the hold being given and the aircraft passing FP.

5 The fact that the hold was not published.

Recommendations

1 Flight crew should be reminded that precise navigation and adequate vertical terrain clearance are of vital importance.

2 When there are any doubts about instructions provided by APP, crews must request clarification before carrying out any manoeuvre based on the information received.

3 ICAO should clarify some ambiguities in its documents, and more specifically in relation to the need to publish all holding circuits and to clarify the standard hold.

British Addendum to Spanish report

The British were, surprisingly, in agreement with the contents of the report by the Spanish accident commission into the accident. Their accredited representative, R G Matthews, felt it necessary though to add the following comments in order to give a proper balance to the Spanish report. This is an abbreviated version:

1 Information regarding the holding pattern at FP, transmitted by ATC, was ambiguous and contributed directly to the disorientation of the crew. The transmission by the captain that the aircraft was taking up the hold at FP was acknowledged by ATC but not queried. In the absence of an instruction to hold this amounted to a tacit approval of the action proposed by the captain and implied that it was what ATC required.

2 The UK interpretation of the criteria detailed in ICAO document 8168 results in a MSA for the procedural entry into the unpublished holding pattern at FP of 7000 feet and for the pattern itself of 6000 feet. Neither of these two figures includes the recommended extra 1000 feet applicable because of the wind effects in hilly terrain. No evidence came to light that, prior to the accident, any MSA calculations had been carried out by a competent authority for this entry and holding pattern. In the absence of a published holding pattern at FP it is reasonable to suppose that the crew would accept the ATC clearance to descend to an altitude of 5000 feet on the assumption that these calculations had been made. It is further evident that if ATC had not cleared the aircraft

below 7000 feet during its attempted entry into the holding pattern, this accident would not have occurred.

3 The 'ideal' track portrayed in Annex A/1 is not practicable, as it is not possible for an aircraft to fly around the sharp angles drawn. A more realistic track over-flying FP would inevitably take the aircraft towards the area of high ground to the south-west of the airfield, this factor must be taken into account when calculating MSAs. TFN is only 6 miles from FP and there is little time in which to intercept the TFN 255° radial before reaching FP. As TFN is equipped with a DME and as no delay was expected it would be quite understandable if the captain decided to fly a flight path which would bring the aircraft overhead FP on a heading of 302° Magnetic, in a good position to carry out the published procedure for landing on runway 12. There is some evidence that this was his intention up to the time ATC passed him the information regarding the hold at FP.

4 It is considered that if the substance of these comments had been reflected in the findings and causes, the report would have been acceptable to the United Kingdom. R G Matthew July 1981.

7

Interpretation

Much of the information we can use to determine the reasons for the destruction of Dan Air 1008 and the deaths of 146 people, came from just two sources; the CVR and the FDR. The FDR was of only a basic type compared to those on modern aircraft today; in fact, for the purposes of the Spanish accident report only 12 parameters were used, and studying these briefly will put in your mind perhaps how the aircraft behaved during its last minutes.

Pitch & Roll

Pitch is the up and down movement of the aircraft nose, controlled by the elevators. Roll is the wing up/down movement, controlled by the ailerons. From the FDR, the roll angle is the first to look at. There appears to be nothing to indicate left or right wing up/down (see 'heading' below for reason). Zero (0) is wings level. At the instance of impact, 1008's wing angle was almost 40°, hence the reason the FE called out 'bank angle.'

Anything greater than 30° is uncomfortable for passengers. The pitch angle was about 5° nose up. Raising the nose does not guarantee the aircraft will climb; generally, it will slow the aircraft slightly – the nose had been held at 1° nose up until just before the crash, when it shot up quickly to 5°.

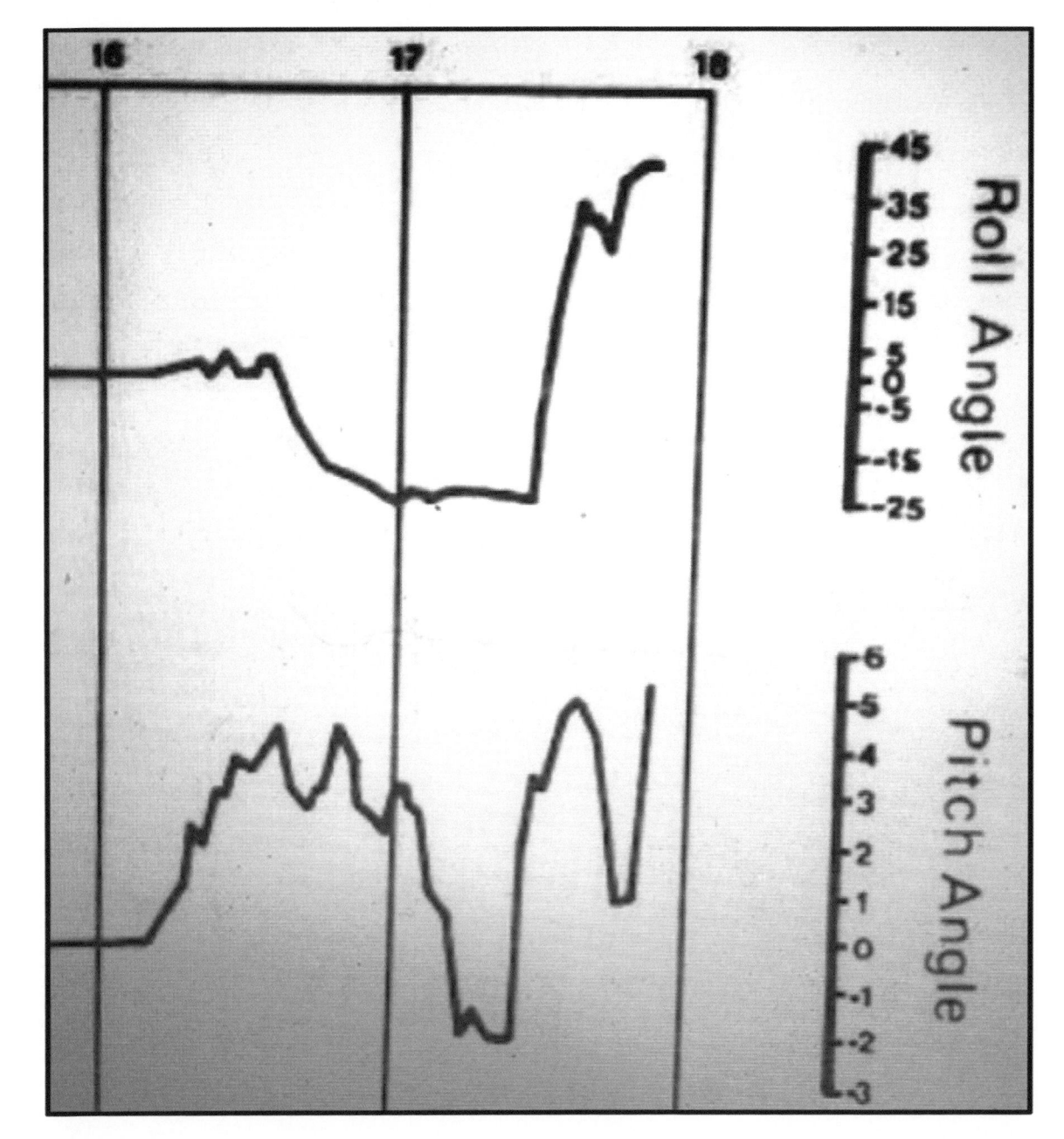

Roll and Pitch angles just prior to collision with the ground (courtesy accident report)

Engine Pressure Ratio (EPRs)

This is the ratio of the turbine discharge pressure, divided by the compressor inlet pressure. In a jet engine, the compressor is at the front, followed by the combustion chambers, then the turbine that powers the compressor via a shaft. EPRs is a means of measuring the amount of thrust produced by an engine.

There is a finite limit on the amount of pressure that an engine is designed to produce. EPRs are used to provide thrust readings to the pilot as the thrust lever is moved in older aircraft. In today's modern equivalent, thrust produced is based on the compressor (or fan) speed and is referred to as N_1.

On Dan Air 1008, the captain calls for his EPRs to be checked as he starts the overshoot procedure. On the FDR, only the two main engines appear to have recorded any ratio, and not the smaller third engine in the tail.

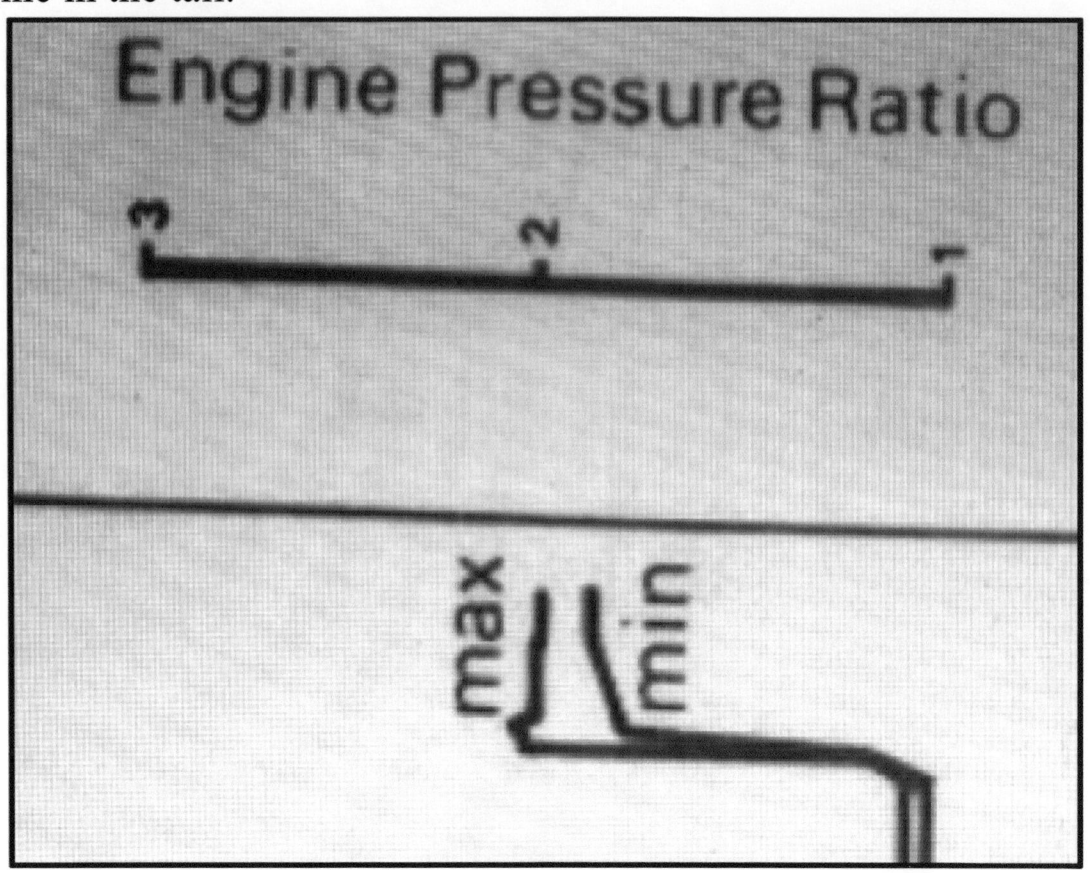

EPRs moments before the crash (courtesy accident report)

The EPRs reading shows normal power still set and not changing, right up to the final moments of the flight, at somewhere just over 1.0. Then suddenly, there is a sharp increase to just below 2.0 on the FDR readout as the overshoot procedure begins.

<u>Vertical Acceleration</u>

This is the indicator of the aircraft's 'g' (gravity) pulled, measured in 'g'. For some reason, this event marker did not start to record until six minutes before the accident, unlike the other parameters.

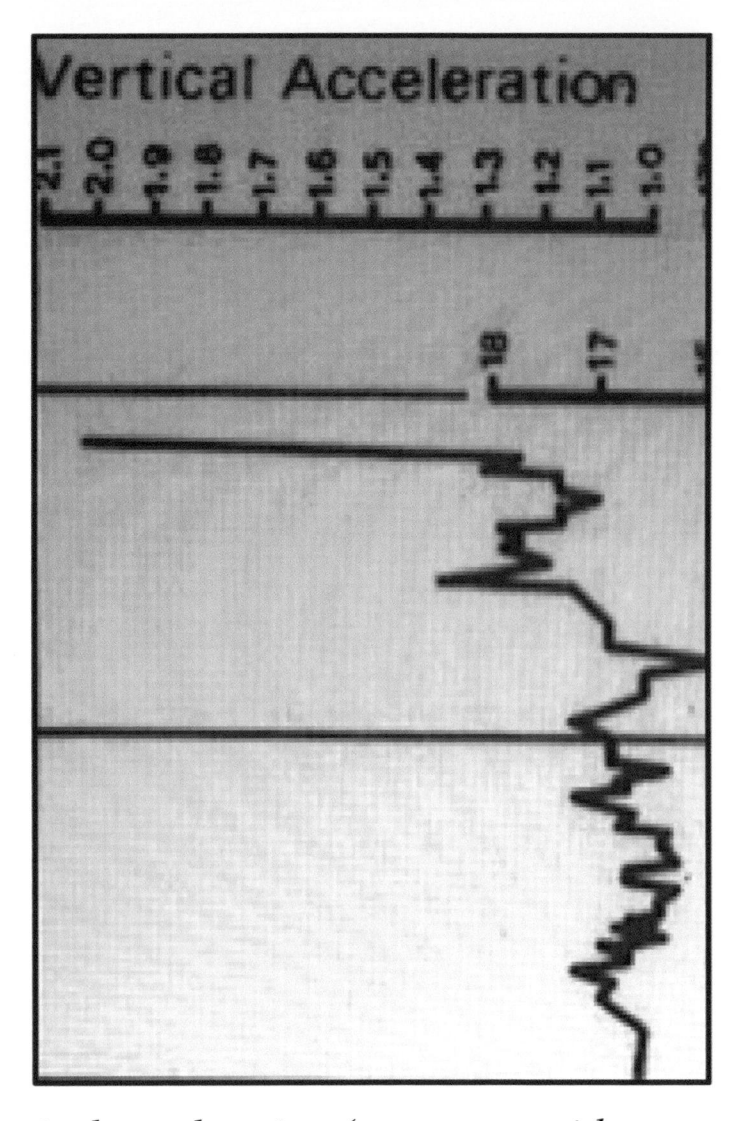

Vertical acceleration (courtesy accident report)

The recording above shows simply the final two minutes of the flight. The top legend shows the vertical acceleration, but there are no units to explain the reference. I believe this is a 'g' reading (gravity) where 1g is normal. Just prior to the crash the 'g' reading was, on average, 1.2g. But the last few seconds show a sudden marked increase to 2.0g, probably as a reaction to the aircraft wing clipping the fog shrouded trees.

Heading, Altitude, Airspeed

The FDR recording for this includes the GWPS alarm on/off markers.

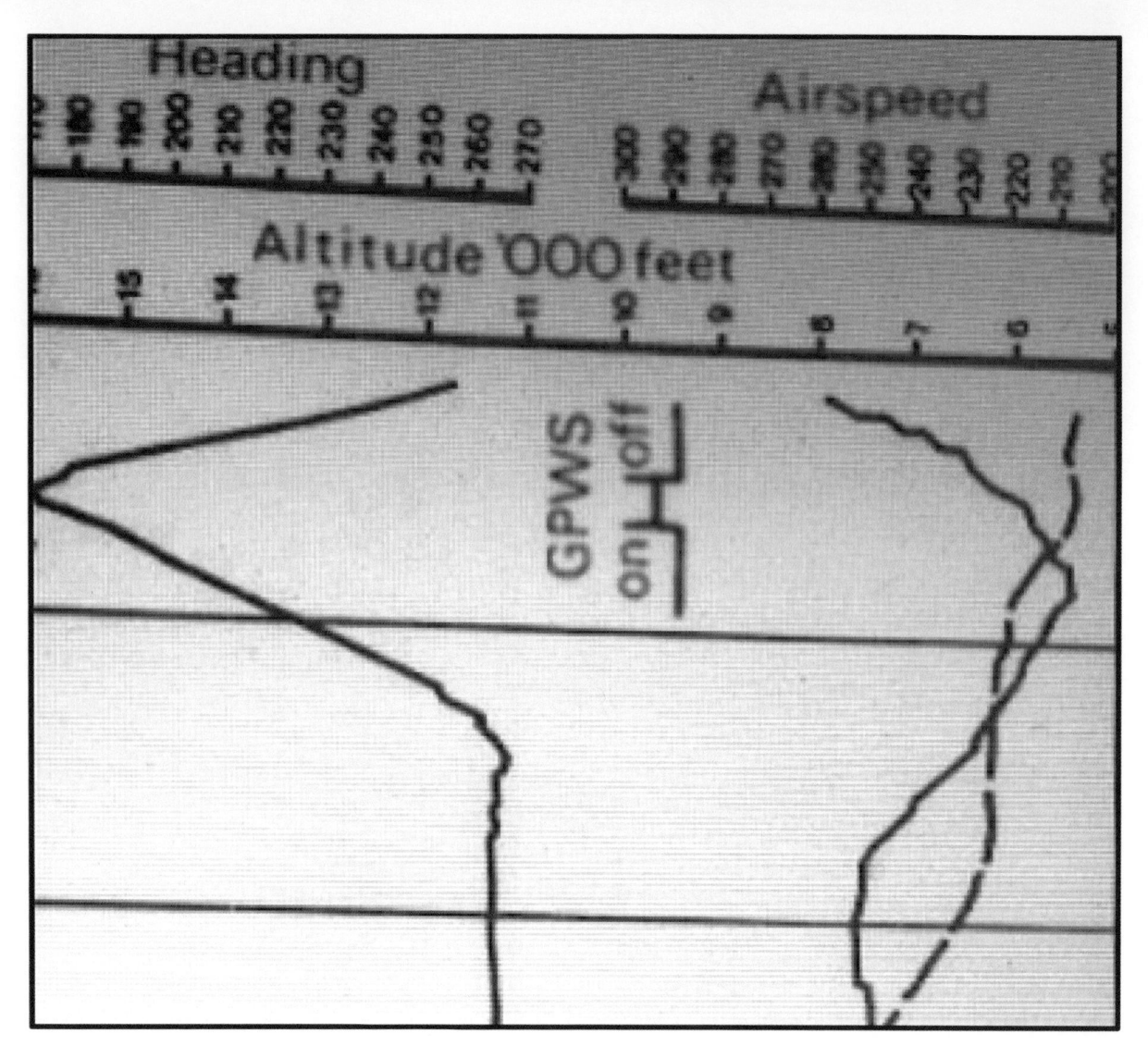

Heading, Altitude, Airspeed, GPWS (courtesy accident report)

Airspeed

These events took a while for me to process. Looking at the chart above, the solid line on the far right, next to the broken line, is the speed line and you have to line that up with the airspeed grid at the top of the page. During the last two minutes, the airspeed decreased from about 250 kts (287 mph) down to a low of about 205 kts (235 mph) before increasing sharply, in line with an increase in EPRs, to about 260 kts (299 mph).

Altitude

This is the broken line above, and shows a gradual descent until two minutes before the accident, where the aircraft levels off at about 6200 feet before, around the moment of GPWS activation, it inexplicably continues to descend to about 5400 at the moment of impact.

Heading

This is the left hand solid line on the chart above. Two minutes before collision with the ground, the aircraft is heading steady on about 260°M (263° M in the text). After about 45 seconds, a left turn is commenced towards 160° on the chart. At the top of the peak, the GPWS activates for about 10 seconds, during which the aircraft banks hard to the right, back towards 260°. This can only be a 'right wing low' roll, as per the roll bullet near the top of this chapter. At nearly 40° of bank the FE called out 'bank angle' to his captain.

Closure Rate (below)

This was recorded in feet/min x 1000, and also a closure rate to terrain in feet/sec. If we start to look at this from 90 seconds before the crash, the aircraft was levelling on its decent to 5000 feet. The rate of closure

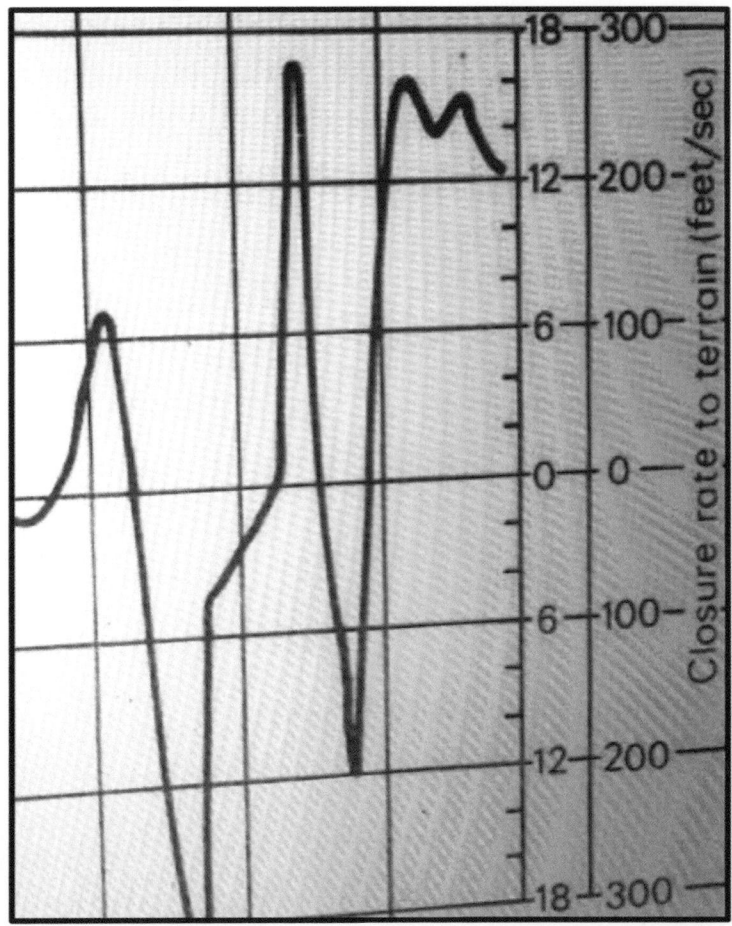

Closure rate for last four minutes (courtesy accident report)

drops when the ground probably fell away – as the aircraft crossed a valley. About 30 seconds from the end, the closure rate increases again as the high ground approaches.

Although the aircraft was banked and not climbing, it is the undulating terrain below that shows the closure rate as it comes up, so to speak, to hit the aircraft at about the equivalent rate of 200 feet/sec. The readings come from a combination of radar altimeter and barometric altimeter.

<u>Height above terrain/aircraft altitude/ground profile (below)</u>
This part of the FDR has three readings upon it: height above terrain (top line), aircraft altitude (middle line) and ground profile (bottom line). At the bottom is also operation of the GPWS.

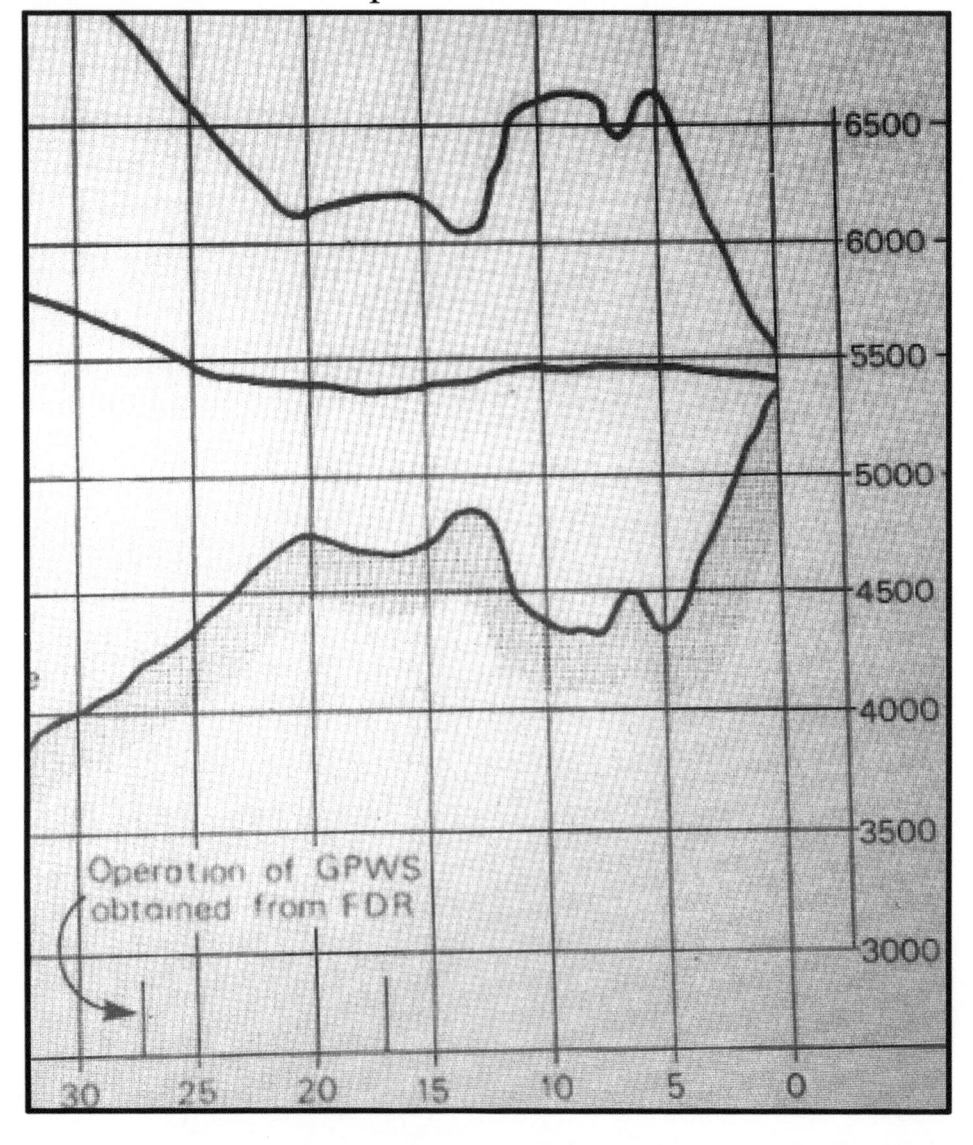

Height/altitude/ground profile (courtesy accident report)

42

Height above terrain

This shows the aircraft height above terrain from its entry at 6500 feet, down to about 5500 feet. Adjustments to altimeter barometric pressure gives a more accurate descent down to about 5450 feet.

Altitude above terrain

The aircraft was descending towards 5000 feet as instructed by ATC when the GPWS warning sounded, and it continued to descend for about a further 2 seconds before the rate of descent was eased, although not stopped altogether. It was only when the GPWS ceased, after a further 7 seconds approximately, that the altitude above terrain increased. This slight increase in altitude, just a mere 15 seconds before the crash, crossed a deep valley and reached a fraction under 5500 feet at its zenith; the aircraft then continued a slight descent, instead of climbing away.

Ground profile

This is fairly obvious. Note the undulations of the terrain and the two marks at the very bottom where the 10 second GPWS warning sounded. The closure rate was such that the alarm sounded about 27 seconds before the crash; although there is a small hill at the 14 second mark, by that time the aircraft had started to climb slightly, hence the GPWS ceased. From about 13 seconds to 3 seconds the aircraft crossed a fairly deep valley, where it levelled off instead of climbing away before descending again; probably due to the steep, right wing down bank causing a loss of altitude. The face of the mountain was simply too steep for a second GPWS warning to happen.

8

What to think?

As I write this, it is more than 37 years since the Dan Air disaster. There is a memorial garden in Manchester and similar at a church on Tenerife. There is nothing at the crash site, because it is too inaccessible and more than a third of a mile from the nearest road. You can't just turn up and go for a walk through the woods in Spain, you know?

In my opinion, memory of this tragic accident has faded fast, although probably not for the families, relatives and friends of the dead. For them, life continues, minus their loved ones. There is much information regarding other air crashes you can read about, but not Dan Air 1008 nor, indeed, the Basle aircraft of 1973, which follows this book.

If you want to know more about the Staines air crash of 1972, in which 118 lives were lost, there is a book. If you want to know about the Zagreb mid-air collision of 1976, in which 176 people were killed, there is book. If you're interested in the Mount Erabus disaster in the Antarctic, in 1979 in which 257 souls perished, there is a book.

So, this is dedicated to the memory of the men and women who did not get to stretch out on a beach in sunny, warm weather, because they died even before stepping out on Spanish soil. We've seen the Spanish accident report and the causes of this tragedy – in Spanish opinion, that the captain, without taking account of the altitude at which he was flying, took his aircraft into an area of high terrain and thereby he failed to maintain a safe height above the terrain as he was required to do. The Spanish did admit that the approach manoeuvre was attempted without having it clearly defined, and also that the hold was not published – minor things against their air traffic controller.

We've also seen the British addendum attached to the Spanish report, in which they say information regarding the holding pattern at FP, transmitted by ATC, was ambiguous and contributed directly to the disorientation of the crew. Also, that MSA calculations had not been done properly and therefore a holding pattern at FP of 7000 feet and the pattern itself at 6000 feet did not include a recommended extra 1000 feet, applicable because of wind effects in hilly terrain, and lastly, the 'ideal' track portrayed in approach plates for the airport were not practicable, since it was not possible for an aircraft to fly around the sharp angles drawn.

So, who was correct? Was the flight crew responsible for the deaths of 146 souls, themselves included, or was it an instruction from ATC that was erroneous, along with a lack of radar and incorrect approach plates regarding MSA? Perhaps the lack of information on the crash of Dan Air 1008 drops a hint that both sides were to blame; Spanish and British?

I'm no pilot, other than a keen Microsoft FSX flight simulator type of pilot. It's clear that the commander of an aircraft is wholly responsible for the operation and safety of his/her's aircraft, just like the captain of a ship. In this, Arthur 'Red' Whelan was sadly deficient that April afternoon. The litany of errors he was responsible for are long.

Pilot errors

1 His first error was to allow 1008 to pass about .79 NMs east of TFN, instead of over it. It's possible the co-pilot could have been flying the aircraft, but nevertheless, any minor infringement should have been pointed out and rectified.

2 He failed to take up the published heading from TFN to FP of 255°.

3 He failed to keep the aircraft's speed under control; was speeding above 250 kts (287 mph) at an altitude requiring him to be under 250 kts, and made little attempt to reduce speed.

4 He did not find enough time, because of his speed, to intercept the FP locator beacon, and missed it by about 1.59 NMs.

5 He failed to turn right towards the FP locator, despite telling ATC he was at FP and taking up the unpublished hold there.

6 He continued on a heading of about 263° whilst descending and still with a high airspeed that would make any manoeuvring towards FP difficult.

7 He and his crew then discussed the unpublished hold, when they were obviously now uncertain of it, and uncertain of their position. He should have radioed ATC for clarification.

8 When cleared by ATC to 5000 feet, he allowed the aircraft to enter a region with a minimum safe altitude (MSA) of 14500 feet. At no time was MSA discussed by the crew; it should have been.

9 He decided the controller's instruction 'inbound 150°, turn to the left' was a tacit instruction to turn left, right away, onto 150° away from FP. He started to turn left, but with a long turn, rather than a tight turn, due to his high airspeed.

10 He suddenly realized that the instruction from ATC meant inbound *towards* FP on a heading of 150° followed by a left turn circuit, and not an immediate turn onto 150°.

11 The GPWS alarm sounded and he decided to overshoot, but did not arrest his descent immediately or climb. He increased engine power (EPRs) but instead of following his co-pilot's advice to turn onto a heading of 122° (which was, it turns out, the overshoot heading for runway 12), he banked sharply to the right.

12 He allowed a 40° bank angle to develop, which resulted in a descent profile and not a climb, and maintained this bank angle until impact with the mountain.

Air traffic errors

Basically, there weren't any major ones! The hold at FP was unpublished, but there was nothing (in 1980) to prevent ATC controllers doing this. He made it quite plain that the hold at FP was inbound 150°, turn to the left. If we must be picky, there are a few minor points that perhaps the controller could have handled better.

1 On hand over from Las Palmas control he mentioned 'no delay,' which perhaps gave the crew of Dan Air the impression there would be no hold up, and so they could hurry on for a quick landing.

2 When informing the crew of the unpublished hold he said 'the standard er, holding overhead FP is…' The crew might have been confused by the sudden mention of a holding pattern overhead FP. It certainly could not be a 'standard holding', as it was unpublished.

3 In all likelihood, mention of this holding pattern led the crew to spend time 'heads down' in the cockpit, trying to find a chart of this holding pattern, but of course there wasn't one, since it was unpublished.

4 As a result of the information received, the crew neglected to check where they were in relation to FP because they were wasting time looking for a plate that did not exist.

5 The controller ends his instruction with 'call you back shortly,' but he never did.

6 It was never made clear to the crew whether they were to actually take up the hold or not. The crew did not query it, nor did the controller query the crew when they advised joining the hold.

7 The controller did not mention any MSA for the area, nor was he obliged to do so, but since he had no radar to assist him it might have been prudent to mention it.

8 When informed that 1008 was taking up the hold, he did not query why; for they were still clear, it seems, to continue their approach, despite IB711 being ahead of them descending for landing.

9 When the controller heard Dan Air announce that they had received a ground proximity warning, he simply replied 'station calling…' but then continued to deal with and clear IB711 to land. It is doubtful there was anything he could have done to help 1008, since he was presuming they were still in the FP holding pattern. Even if he had radar, the tall mountains to the south-west of the airfield would likely obstruct any view of a radar paint (echo).

What I think

Sadly, there are just slightly more errors on the part of the flight crew compared to that of ATC, and those of the controller cannot be directly attributed to what happened on 25th April 1980. I understand both Spain and the UK would want to exonerate their own parties from blame for this tragedy, but most aircraft accidents are the result of an accumulation of mistakes by a number of parties or factors.

From the flight crew: inaccurate navigation from the approach to TFN; inaccurate heading from TFN to FP; airspeed too fast for an approach considering the short distance between the two navaids; the mistake in not understanding the unpublished FP holding instructions and especially, the 'turn to the left' which resulted in the captain immediately commencing a left turn; failure to check their flight charts and notice the MSA ahead of them was 14500 feet; failure to arrest their descent when the GPWS activated and climb away; holding a bank angle of about 40° that resulted in a still continuous but gentle descent, and lastly, not querying the controller's instructions for his unpublished hold at FP.

From the air traffic controller: using the words 'no delay' then announcing an unpublished 'advisory' holding pattern overhead FP and using the words 'turn to the left' rather than 'turns to the left'; not querying the aircraft high speed nor why he was taking up the advisory hold in the first place; not announcing the MSA for the region, and not having radar, which was not, of course, his fault.

Sadly, for the 138 fare paying passengers on board Dan Air 1008, and the 5 cabin staff who looked after them, their lives were snuffed out in an instant on a Spanish mountain due to the incompetence at that moment of the flight crew assisted by the Spanish air traffic controller, his unpublished holding pattern, and a lack of suitable radar in the region.

In my Volume II, I will examine the demise of Invicta 435 from the UK, a Vickers Vanguard turboprop, that crashed into a snowy Swiss mountain in April 1973, killing 108 women and children, but with 37 survivors. Read how the French tried to wiggle out of that one, when in fact it was illegal radio transmissions that lured Invicta 435 to its destruction.

INDEX

1

1008, 2, 3, 4, 5, 6, 8, 9, 10, 11, 12, 13, 14, 15, 16, 18, 19, 20, 21, 25, 28, 30, 31, 32, 36, 38, 44, 45, 47, 48

A

ADF, 6, 27
APP, 8, 9, 12, 13, 14, 16, 17, 18, 20, 34
Arthur John Whelan, 5
ATC, 6, 13, 25, 26, 27, 28, 30, 32, 33, 34, 35, 43, 45, 46, 48
ATPL, 5

B

Birmingham, 5
Boeing 727, 4, 5, 6

C

CPL, 5
CVR, 23, 25, 36

D

DME, 6, 9, 25, 35

E

EPR, 19

F

FB, 11, 15
FDR, 23, 25, 32, 36, 38, 39, 42
FE, 9, 13, 15, 16, 17, 19, 27, 28, 30, 36, 41
FP, 10, 11, 16, 17, 25, 26, 27, 28, 29, 30, 31, 32, 33, 34, 35, 45, 46, 47, 48

G

G-BDAN, 4
GPWS, 18, 19, 22, 24, 28, 30, 32, 40, 41, 42, 43, 46, 48
Grand Canary, 8, 23

H

Hapag-Lloyd 542, 13

I

IB711, 13, 20, 25, 31, 32, 47
Iberia 711, 13, 17, 18, 20
ILS, 6, 12, 13, 19, 20, 23, 28
ITF, 13, 23

J

Justo Camin Yanes, 15, 25

L

Las Palmas, 8, 9, 23, 25, 31, 47
Los Rodeos, 5, 6, 11, 17, 20, 23

M

Manchester airport, 4, 6
Michael John Firth, 5
MSA, 21, 26, 27, 28, 30, 31, 34, 45, 46, 47, 48

P

P1, 12, 13, 15, 16, 18, 19
P2, 12, 13, 15, 16, 17, 18, 19
Pico del Chiriguel, 21

Q

QFE, 9, 12, 18, 28
QNH, 9, 18, 28

R

radio altimeter, 6, 24
Raymond John Carey, 5

S

South Cemetery, 4

T

Tenerife, 2, 3, 4, 5, 8, 9, 13, 20, 21, 44
TFN, 9, 10, 11, 13, 14, 15, 25, 26, 29, 30, 31, 32, 33, 35, 45, 48
transponder, 6

V

VLF Omega, 6
VOR, 9, 10, 11, 13, 15, 31

Printed in Great Britain
by Amazon